MCGREGOR, GRISELDA SARAH
Grit, growth and
sometimes groovy:
Aberdeen in the 60s

AaD1

220159

GRIT
GROWTH
AND SOMETIMES
GROOVY

ABERDEEN IN THE 60s

GRISELDA SARAH McGREGOR

Keith Murray Publications

Published by Keith Murray Publications,
46 Portal Crescent, Tillydrone, Aberdeen,
Scotland AB2 2SP

First published March 1990

Printed by Astra Printing Services,
43-47 Jopps Lane, Aberdeen

Edited and designed by Graham MacLennan
and Jim Stewart

© Griselda Sarah McGregor 1990

ISBN 1 870978 23 4

The publisher gratefully acknowledges the following
sources for the use of their photographs for
reproduction in this book:

For their help and support, I wish to thank
Scotpix, Studio Morgan, Aberdeen University
Library's private collection, Aberdeen City
Library, Aberdeen Art Gallery & Museums,
Hulton Picture Library, Aberdeen Football Club,
St Andrews University's photographic
collection, D.C.Thomson & Company Ltd,
BP Photographic Library, Mr Allan White, Mr
Peter Cruickshank, Mr Steve Robertson,
Alison MacKintosh, Mr Graeme Munro, Mrs
Margaret Murray, Mrs Margaret Duncan and
Mr Ally Walker.
   Also, for her encouragement and faith over
many years, I am indebted to my late mother,
Dr Margaret Sarah McGregor.

Griselda Sarah McGregor

Aberdeen-born Griselda Sarah McGregor is a languages graduate of Aberdeen University and feels very much a child and "graduate" of the Sixties. After university, she travelled abroad mainly in the countries where the languages she had studied — French, German and Russian — were spoken.

It was during her sojourn to the USSR that she began writing of her impressions and experiences of people and places. It also decided her on a literary rather than languages career.

On her return to the UK she went to live in Dundee where she worked as a photo-journalist with D.C. Thomson & Company Ltd for 17 years. One unexpected and still largely unexplained accolade of this period was a medal for merit in journalism awarded by the American Legion.

She has recently re-established her roots in the North-east, where she works on a freelance basis. She keeps up her interests in poetry and foreign languages and has been enjoying brushing up on another favourite language — the Doric.

Uncluttered with humanity, Union Street's buildings wore
their fine facades with almost sartorial elegance.

The Sixties may not have brought quite the same "swinging
scene" to Aberdeen as they did to London. Nevertheless, the
decade saw the Granite City swing with sometimes ponderous
but very positive momentum into a new era, changing the city's face
and pace.

Beneath the stolidly-handsome facade, there were the rumblings
(often accompanied by grumblings) of progress. New buildings,
civic, commercial, residential, glittering with glass, sprang up to
tower incongruously above their Victorian, Edwardian and squat pre-
war neighbours. The oil industry that was to flood the city in the
Seventies was already an inexorable trickle, the "boom" a not-too-
distant rat-tat-tat.

While oil was to cause a population explosion of incomers,
Aberdeen's medical efforts and strategies brought a significant fall in
the birth rate — one of the lowest in Britain — thanks to widespread
prescription of the contraceptive pill. Apart from the obvious
benefits, it was a controversial topic of the period. A "new morality"
was born, liberating, sometimes bewildering for the young, shocking
to many of the older generations.

For those in teens and twenties it was an exciting time of
revolution in pop music (spearheaded by the Beatles), in fashion,
cult heroes and general mores. In the later Sixties, hair grew long,
flowers and beads of seeds sprouted on outlandish gear, bells

1

The Dee (above) and Don (opposite) mouthes as they were spanned in 1960, with vehicular transport a very distant rumble from today's temper-fraying trauma of trundling traffic. No real worries over fume pollution here unless it was from the reeking lums of industry on the horizon.

tinkled. Flower Power was here and an earlier generation shook its head in dismay, as it has always done. Discotheques and boutiques blossomed, many but briefly.

There were the dramas of an epidemic which kept Aberdeen in the national headlines for many weeks — creating an almost wartime fighting spirit of camaraderie — a sensational murder trial and several winters of severe hardship. It was a time when pleasure and leisure activities were simple, and holidays were still taken largely in and around the city. For the majority, the lure and availability of the "Costa dels" was yet to come.

Cinema, theatre and "the dancin'" were the popular diversions for Saturday night. Eating out was still in the Special Occasion bracket. No quick trips to the video shop. Seeing a film meant a proper outing, often starting at the wrong end of a lengthy queue.

Theatre-goers were divided. There was the ethnic humour, song and dance of the Tivoli down by the harbour in Guild Street and rather more up-market entertainment from His Majesty's Theatre.

Not only Sixties fledglings, but generations before, fluttered through their first dancing steps under the eagle-eyed tutelage of the legendary Madame Murray. On Saturday afternoons, in the hall behind the Cowdray Hall, this formidable lady held rigorous relays of classes for schoolboys and girls.

On Saturday nights, Madame held a dance no less sternly chaperoned by herself. Who one might meet as "Madame's" was one of the anticipatory pleasures of Saturday.

Apprenticeship served, young folk graduated to larger, less-sheltered venues. The glamorous lights and central revolving orb of the Palace Ballroom (off Bridge Street) drew like a magnet. Cheaper and smaller was the well-patronised Palais in Diamond Street and even more democratic, the huge Beach Ballroom drawing dancers by the busload. ("See you inside" was an all-too-frequent date-making invitation!)

Saturday night hops at "the Mitch" — the university's Mitchell Hall within Marischal College quadrangle — had the attraction of a faint hint of Bohemia.

A time-honoured activity on socially-restricted Sunday evenings was "walkin' the mat", a youthful promenading of Union Street, up one side, down the other. News and gossip were exchanged while eyes ever scanned the passing throng for "talent" of the opposite sex.

The first Chinese restaurant, the Bamboo in Union Street, created a considerable stir with its strange fare and flocked wallpaper. A meal there was an outing in itself, not as today, a suffix to an evening's entertainment. The only "take-away" was a pair of chopsticks inscrutably presented to the departing diner.

The promenade in 1960, sparse of private vehicles but lined with public transport, the most popular mode for seaside-seekers.

With the dearth of collision-course crowds (on feet or on wheels) Aberdeen's architectural aplomb shone forth.

A Union Street more busy, but still more busy
with buses than anything else. The old
Capitol cinema, below the flags on the right,
saw many famous pop groups of the day play
to houses of hysteria. The Rolling Stones
appeared there in 1964, eliciting all the
screaming, fainting and body-hurls stage-
wards which had by then become trademarks
of contemporary musical appreciation.

A Union Street still devoid of today's traffic hold-ups.

One kind of traffic hold-up no-one minded. The circus coming to town was an ever-popular crowd-drawer. (Note the conspicuous absence of animal rights protesters — as yet!)

Even the limb-flinging posture of the 18th century statue of William Wallace seems to invite admiration for an impressive, albeit incongruous threesome, the City Libraries, St Mark's Church and His Majesty's Theatre, long and affectionately dubbed "Education, Salvation and Damnation".

Holburn Junction — a time-honoured meet-
ing place as, sooner or later, buses from
most parts of the city and hinterlands must
pass through. For longer waits and colder
weather, the Mitsouku, an early coffee bar
(just out of vision on the right) provided
congenial shelter.

A quiet summer's day at Union Terrace Gardens with His Majesty's Theatre in the background. As well as being famous for their formal floral displays, the gardens were the scene for many organised events during summer months. In July, 1969, Aberdeen Links and Parks department held an "Aberdeen Summer Girl" charm contest. Perhaps in mild protest at all the liberty, egality and nudity going on elsewhere, bikinis and swimsuits were banned. The prim entry regulations stated "Summer dresses only"!

There can be few, Aberdonian or otherwise, who escaped the lens of the Union Street photographer. The camera-shy might attempt to dodge or cross over, but it was as well to give in gracefully. Sooner or later, you'd be "captured" for posterity, hopefully in your Saturday best . . . but often more informally attired.

Sadly these roving recorders proved to be an endangered species and by the end of the Sixties had vanished from the streets.

The Timmer Market

The Timmer Market's original lure — all goods of solid woods — had palled by the Sixties, when lurid plastics and parrots became the brightly-coloured eye-catchers. A photograph of oneself with pirate-style parrot on shoulder was, apparently, a much sought after souvenir. Shiver me timmers!

Tiny monkeys were also pressed into service as photographic props, a practice eventually discontinued out of consideration to the creatures and the folk posing with them. Not infrequently, peck-tetchy parrot and monkey failed to see eye to eye, with a resultant flurry of feathers and fur.

Entering the Green from any angle was a delight to the eyes and nose. The ancient, colourful market co-existed flourishingly with ever-increasing super-markets right through the decade. Sadly, it lost much of its "vigour" in the Seventies.

The Cowdray Hall and war memorial with its
granite lion sentinel.

Lament for Henry.
A dialogue while
walking the mat

Losh Dod! Fit's adae wi' peer Henry?
Ah'm feart he's gan saft in the heid.
Ah says: "Are ye gan tae the Palais?"
An' he says: "Na, Ah'm gan tae ma bed."

Ah spied him frae the Monkey Hoose ae nicht —
the rain wis jist fair stottin' doon.
He wis gawpin' in jewellers' shop windies,
files heavin' great sighs at the meen.

He's jist nae the same loon that he wis, Jake,
an' Jake, fan Ah sa him astreen
Ah says: "There's a pairty at Bella's."
an he says: "Ach, Ah'm no awfy keen."

It's a gey queer turn that he's te'en
for a lad fa aye played big and teuch.
Man, a terrible notion's jist flashed through ma heid —
Dod, ye dinna think Henry's in LOVE!

Griselda Sarah McGregor

The children's village (above). The Aberdeen beach adventure playground, opened in June, 1962, was one of the first of its kind in the country and hailed as imaginative in design . . . and virtually indestructible.

A summery summary of Aberdeen's attractions (top left). A period postcard showing some of the city's aspects of interest and industry. It was in the early Sixties that Aberdeen's inspired tourist-orientated parenthesis was first coined — "The silver city by the golden sands".

A bathing belle (bottom left) in a fetchingly-daring swimsuit for 1960. What is perhaps more breathtaking was that the young lady was taking a first daring dip of the year — in early March in a temperature of 47 degrees F!

A crowded summer scene at Aberdeen beach in the mid-Sixties — later to be reproduced in duty-free droves and the Costa crush. Three foreground lads seem content viewing the attractions of "home-grown talent". Note the youngsters stripped off for a "dook", while canny elders hang on to coats and cardies.

The beach "au naturelle", however, still provided youngsters with all the facilities they required. Two lads — and a dog — had the bonus of an unexpected "trial" with an off-duty Denis Law, then Britain's most expensive soccer star. Law, too, had been a fitba' daft schoolboy, spotted for stardom at a time when he couldn't afford to buy his own football boots.

The ephemeral flowering domes of summer umbrellas lend a continental flavour to Hazlehead restaurant (above).

In 1961, Hazlehead Park saw the renaissance of Aberdeen Highland Games, where Bill Anderson showed his skills (bottom right). Then described as "a Bucksburn athlete", he went on to become an internationally-famous "heavy".

Highland dancers go through their paces at the games (bottom left).

Get lost! . . . no problem at Hazlehead maze,
the only problem was getting out.

The attraction
of traction

The annual traction engine rally held at the links drew Sixties seekers of a nostalgic glimpse into the past. The rally's venue was later moved to Hazlehead. Behind the foreground engine's chimney is another "nostalgic" chimney — that of the old Beach baths, built in the late 19th Century and finally demolished in 1973.

The rather pretty fashions of the late Fifties and early Sixties with tight-fitting waists and full skirts frothed out with frilly paper nylon petticoats faded and died like full-blown roses. The mini skirt, all straight lines and brevity marched in. Many a buxom body was bullied by its owner into the necessary angularity. As hemlines shot upwards, so boots lengthened — to bridge the gap as it were — long, tall cousins of the neat little ankle boots they superceded.

The Gentle Germination of Flower Power

The flowers in our hair, the bells, beads and bangles,
cohorts of kaftans and brown leather sandals . . .
strange twangy music of Eastern notes,
"macrobiota" and Afghan coats . . .
an aura of incense, Peace, Loving to all
came early one summer
and died the next fall.

The candles went out, but some hardy annuals
(found in each cult) persevere to this day.
I guess "born again" hippies
are here to stay.

Griselda Sarah McGregor

The mini it was, too, which sounded the death knell of stockings and suspenders, a passing much lamented in male quarters.

Rigid "beehives" gave way to centre partings and long, straight manes. If nature had not obliged with straight hair, good results could be cheaply, if uncomfortably, achieved by bending down, laying your locks on the ironing board and giving them a quick run over with a steam iron.

For all the clone-like followers of fashion, there were always the few who stood out from the crowd. This Castlegate fashion plate of a city gent (above) was actually an unemployed labourer. Devoting his increased free time to keeping up appearances and indulging his passion for fashion earned him the nickname "the dandiest dude in the dole queue"!

Groovy gents who were still shortish, if not back-and-sided, greatly favoured roll-neck sweaters and the innovation of the polo-neck shirt (right).

Spring beauties at the students' charities
flower stall in St Andrew's Church square in
Union Street. Their flower power predates
that in San Francisco by almost five years.

Crown Street Revisited

My lost Bohemia!
Quartier Latin of my youthful student days.
Do they still aim to set society ablaze
through new thoughts, and put all things right
with talk and instant coffee in the night?

With those interminable cups,
hot, stimulating, black,
do they pursue the existential quest
for what we lack?

And is it just a phase,
like duffle coats and jeans?
Oh Hirsute, hopeful Youth
which sought to blaze the trail
with Reformation's flame!

While lesser mortals sleep,
do they still plumb the depths and delve
into the Mind, go to bed at three —
crawl blinking forth at twelve?

Do they still aim
to change the world . . .

. . . then only change themselves?

Griselda S. McGregor

The Queen and the Duke of Edinburgh
with Principal T.M. Taylor at the official
opening of Crombie Hall, Aberdeen
University's first hall of residence, on
Saturday, August 16, 1960.

These jolly jokers "persuaded" their unfortunate vehicle all the way along the Deeside railway line — fortunately by that time closed down! It was all, of course, in the cause of charity.

Fun Raising and Fundraising

For town and gown alike. there were two highlights in rag-week. the student show performed at His Majesty's Theatre and on the last evening. the "torcher". a torchlit procession of colourful floats and folk through the town. The student revue's high standards are reflected in the fact that a now-famous show-business trio made their "Scotland the What?" debut in an early Sixties student show (top left).

Then came the grand finale. the Charities Ball which included a sort of beauty contest. the crown going to the "Spirit of the Arts". Student antics apart. solo long-distance walks were a much-favoured means of fund-raising in the Sixties. This hardy Highlander (bottom left) chose to tow his "cairtie" all the way from Inverness to Aberdeen.

Catering for 46 men and 64 women, Crombie Hall was the first hall in the country to accommodate male and female students — but cautiously included the facility of single-sex common rooms as well as mixed.

Prior to the advent of Crombie, incomer students relied for the most part on a large "army" of landladies who kept all-in accommodation rooms — and a watchful, motherly eye on their young charges, the latter not always appreciated as much as the former! There were also "bed-sit brigades" in many parts of the city.

The streamlined beginnings of Aberdeen
University's third hall of residence, Dunbar Hall,
late in 1965, as yet dwarfed by the elegant
contrast of King's College Chapel spire. Dunbar
Hall was later to win a Civic Trust award and
praise for a design toning so well with the
ancient character of the 18th Century Chanonry
of Old Aberdeen.

King's College bus-stop.
Winter afternoon.

A straggling queue they gather there.
An aimless cluster, ruffling, hunched against the air,
those few who leave between hours
devoid of that instinctive senseless haste
which makes you run as if all Hell
were after you.

Black perched along the wall, silent against the cold,
they stand and turn in long dark coats and twining scarves.
A lonely one or two, a small crowd, huddling, dense
flapping sombre arms anon . . .
Black crows upon a fence.

Griselda Sarah McGregor

39

The Queen, Prince Andrew, Princess Anne and Prince Charles greeted by Lord Provost Norman Hogg after disembarking from the Royal Yacht Britannia in the summer of 1965.

Bottom left — Shyly smiling, a demure Princess Ann disembarks from the Royal Yacht Britannia at Aberdeen for the summer hols at Balmoral in August, 1961 . . . clearly before the days when strained relations with the media were to earn her the nickname, albeit briefly, of "Her Royal Rudeness".

Bottom right— The Queen Mother in August, 1963, visiting the gracious "salons" of Bells Antiques shop in Bridge Street. Curiously, the premises are today occupied by Central Computers Ltd, a company specialising in all the technology of the future.

Aberdeen (then Dyce) Airport, 1960. Not the sunniest year of the Sixties, but Queen Elizabeth the Queen Mother could always be counted on for a warm smile invariably reciprocated by often-sodden waiting crowds. The Queen Mother is seen (opposite) leaving for Balmoral.

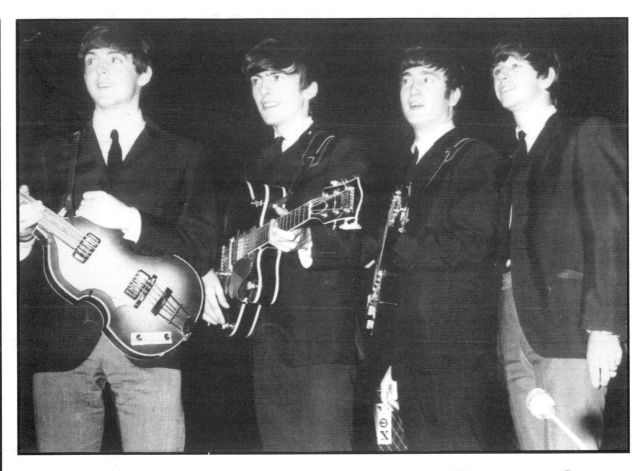

Things Start to Swing

The pop music scene rollicked and rolled through the decade with joyous, just occasionally slightly aggressive abandon. The schmaltzy, croony days of the Fifties were ousted by times a-changing; much new and original composition and presentation, a louder beat — and "louder" clothes.

In January, 1963, folk flocked to the Beach Ballroom to see the Johnny Scott Band Show featuring an odd-looking and sounding quartet from Liverpool — the Beatles, then nicknamed the "Love me do boys" after their first big hit. There were few screaming teenies for the latter; not hordes but a handful sought their autographs. Nevertheless, Aberdonians shelled out 3/- for this the "Fab Four's" first and last appearance in the city.

Viewed with hindsight, group publicity shots
show touchingly tidy young chaps and a
determined effort at uniformity which wouldn't
now look out of place in an insurance office.
The East Coast Flames (above), doing their bit
to set the heather alight, were already sporting
early Beatle cuts and "groovy gear" . . .

. . . while two members of the Commancheros, seen at a wedding, show a definite Shadows influence.

Nearer home and nearer Grandpop than pop, Jimmy Shand, perhaps Scotland's most famous band leader, announced on a short tour of the North-east that he had no intention of retiring, ever, as long as there were folk who wanted to hear his music. He had then been in showbusiness for over 40 years.

This local hero (now incidentally a highly-respectable graphic designer) projects his own eclectic image based perhaps on Roy Orbison, Buddy Holly, Gene Vincent, James Dean . . . He admits his idol days were short-lived, beginning while a schoolboy and ending while a student. Ironically, his equally short-lived group was called The Who, and were performing long before the other Who found fame.

Young lady with an identity crisis?
The Mods and Rockers of the early Sixties clashed sartorially as well as physically — remember Clacton when rival Rocker bikers and moped-mounted Mods brought gang warfare to the sleepy seaside streets?

This Mod-clad girl appears to be fraternising with the opposition.

Unkempt beginnings in 1965 for St Nicholas
House, the city's new £2 million municipal offices
looked down upon by the elegantly-groomed and
very definitely-completed Marischal College.
Although the first municipal department had
"flitted" into the new headquarters by the late
Sixties, the official "christening", performed by
Scottish Secretary William Ross, was not held
until May 1, 1970. It was a particularly proud
occasion for city architect George Keith, who was
to retire shortly afterwards. St Nicholas House
was one of the outstanding features of the
considerable role Mr Keith played in the design
of post-war Aberdeen.

Contrasting constructions in the vertical. Sharp foreground perpendiculars of the children's amusement park at the beach with the hazy shape of the new Gallowgate flats looming on the horizon alongside spectral spires.

The Gallowgate flats — and a new lifestyle — coming into closer focus.

But the proud and peaceful solidity of private
dwellings was still to be found . . . in this case at
Albert Street, near the Grammar School, seen
in the background.

The then dramatically "futuristic" dome of the
new Natural Philosophy building in Old
Aberdeen (now renamed the Fisher Noble
building), which was opened by Sir George
Paget Thomson, FRS, in May, 1964.

Two schools on two hills. These very different
buildings house two of Aberdeen's schools of
distinction.

Above — Robert Gordon's College, Schoolhill.

Below — The Medical School, Foresterhill, then
said to be architecturally and functionally the
best of its kind in the country.

A different kind of "high-rise building" in the mid-Sixties, when Hall Russell, shipbuilders, was still a name synonymous with mighty growth, before it sadly ceased to be the institution it was for generations.

A damp day but a sunny send-off for the Conqueror from the launching party. For the ladies, hats, gloves — and handbags — were clearly de rigeur for so formal an occasion.

Set Fair to Shape Futures

The Malcolm Miller, the Sail Training Association's topsail schooner built at the Torry shipyard of John Lewis & Sons, spread her canvas for the first time on February 13, 1968. The three-masted schooner, sister ship to the Sir Winston Churchill and costing £175,000, carries 7100 square feet of sail when fully rigged.

This Sail Training Association's project aimed to offer "character-building training aboard the ship" to young folk from all walks of life.

The ship was named the Malcolm Miller in memory of the son of Sir James Miller, a well-known Edinburgh businessman. Sir James offered to finance the building of this second Sail Training Association vessel following the tragic death of his son Malcolm, then in his mid-twenties, as a result of a rallying accident.

Opposite page — Shipyard cranes echo the graceful mast structure of the Malcolm Miller at rest in the harbour.

Quarantined — but the message gets through.

The Beleaguered City

An outbreak of typhoid in May, 1964, made Aberdeen of nationwide, fever-pitch interest as victim numbers escalated in the following weeks. Variously described by the media as a "stunned", "beleaguered" and "ghost" city, its citizens showed a determined cheeriness and "kept right on" spirit one would expect of the stalwart Aberdonians.

As the centre for an agricultural community, Aberdeen was not unfamiliar with the state of quarantine. Earlier in the Sixties, an outbreak of foot and mouth disease decimated cattle herds in the North-east and called a similar if less-drastic halt to any social gatherings for those connected with farming or handling animals.

Aberdeen City Hospital. Alfresco typhoid patients.

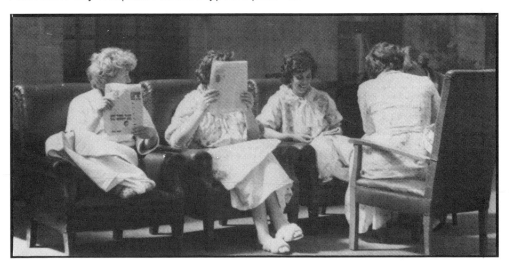

Plastic gloves, food-handling tongs, facilities for between-sales hand-washing appeared almost overnight in shops and were embraced with much enthusiasm. However the practice seemed to wither and die almost as soon as the epidemic.

An Aberdeen Cleansing Department lorry disinfects Union Street. Similar trucks trundled all main streets. Presumably typhoid bugs shunned side streets.

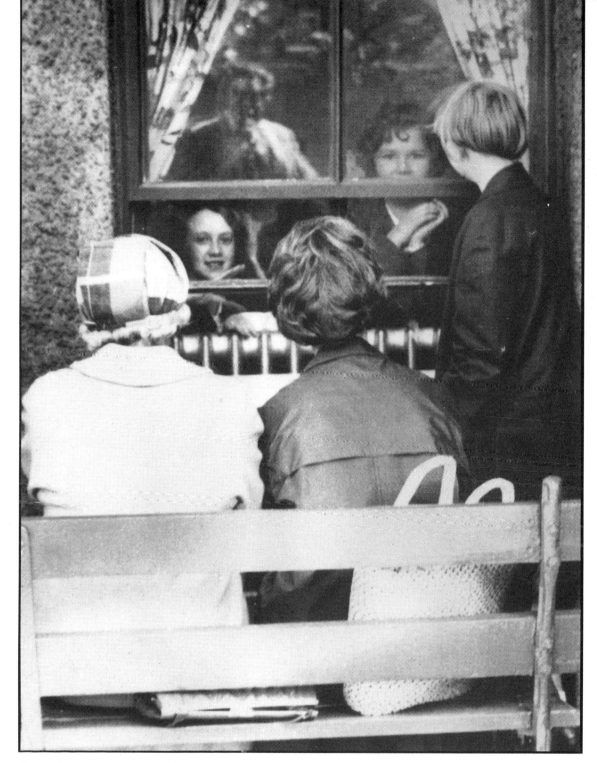

For patients young and old, this was as
close as they would get to family and
friends for weeks.

Apart from these cheery hospital huddles of fellow victims, the kirk on Sunday provided the only opportunity for gatherings of folk in the "beleaguered city".

Friends and relatives visited faithfully during the epidemic, but, sometimes, something — like posing for a Press photographer — would brighten the long hours of windowsill perching.

The outbreak brought glee for youngsters as schools held classes out of doors — then finally closed. An unusually fine spell of weather followed and children spared the disease — tanned and super-fit through the liberty of a bonus holiday — provided an ironic, sharper contrast to their pallid relatives and contemporary victims.

Aberdeen's fine medical reputation was amplified by the swift containment of the epidemic. There were, of course, those of the old brigade who claimed that cure came fastest from our pure, fresh air and sunshine.

The source of infection was traced to part of a consignment of corned beef from South America. Dr Ian MacQueen, Aberdeen's Medical Officer for Health, was later awarded the OBE for his handling of the crisis — though local wags rumoured it ought to have been the CBE — "Corned Beef Exterminator"!

Murder most foul — and fascinating

Not a cinema queue! The sensational murder trial of Mrs Sheila Garvie in November, 1966 (ending in her conviction) drew larger crowds than any cinema or theatre box office hit.

Based on an eternal love triangle, the plot, as it unfolded, proved more dramatic and convoluted than any crime fiction, shocking yet fascinating its followers.

Other key characters in this sorry scenario were the lover, Brian Tevendale and equally important, but absent, farmer Maxwell Garvie, the murdered husband.

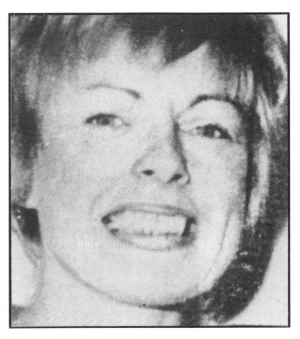

Mrs Sheila Garvie in earlier, happier times.

Another "high drama" news picture — the
Clydesdale bank in Union Street which was
the scene of a robbery.

"Driver rescued . . . later allowed home."
A mangled but not demolished Morris 1000, a
slightly dented bus (bound for Torry). This
newsworthy accident shot seems quaintly tame
compared with most of today's horror crashes.

Shock tactics of wreckage "sculpture" and
macabre puns were among police efforts to
improve road safety in the late Sixties. This
tattered tableau greeted visitors to County
Police headquarters at Bucksburn.

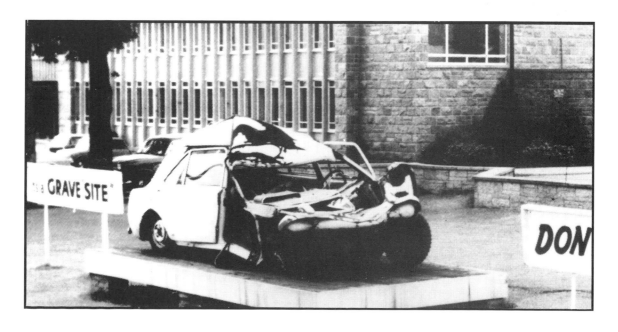

An almost balletic arrangement of arms, legs and bodies — could it be an example of the "Fix the Ba'" competition?

The Thinking Man's Football Club

The most popular theory as to the origin of Aberdeen Football Club's nickname, the Dons, is that it owes nothing to the River Don but refers to the large proportion of founder members belonging to the teaching profession when the club was inaugurated in 1881.

The ground, originally known as Pittodrie Park after the owner of the land, Mr Knight Erskine of Pittodrie, was "promoted" to Pittodrie Stadium in the Sixties, following a £100,000 facelift.

A wintry Pittodrie Stadium stand peopled with well-clad spectators — looking not unlike a colony of Emperor penguins in Antartica. "Bunneted" and thick-coated, they contrast curiously with their scantily-clad heroes, the Dons and their opponents.

The new decade kicked off to a flying start for Aberdeen FC. The Dons are here seen with manager Eddie Turnbull in April, 1970, the year they won the Scottish Cup.

Grim seas and an anxious audience as a
rocket line is fired from the shore to the
Grimsby trawler Ross Fortune in distress off
the mouth of the Don.

A cruel sea crumbles the defences of
Stonehaven harbour.

Late for work again! The morning after a heavy
fall in December, 1969.

Of course, "bad" was "good" for the skiers,
sending them scampering happily to the slopes.
Chairlift-borne fellow pupils at Gordonstoun,
Prince Charles and Prince Guelf of Hanover
prepare to enjoy a day on the Cairngorms.

There was plenty of time and opportunity for fun too. Despite school closures, these youngsters weren't at a loose end to find an original way of clearing their garden, drive and street while amusing themselves at the same time. Result — one 17'2" snowman "sculpture".

It took a hardy Aberdonian, Sandra Rennie, to choose a swimsuit for sledging on the slopes at Abergeldie. Scots actor John Gregson, then appearing in Breaking Point at His Majesty's Theatre, looks positively overdressed!

December, 1969, and in Swinging London, a
dozen Father Christmases (three of them, in
fact, Mother Christmases) were remanded on
bail of £50 each when they appeared at
Marlborough Street Court.

The 12, all members of the Santa Claus
Union, had been arrested outside an Oxford
Street store protesting against the exploitation
of children's fantasies by stores which charged
for Santa's presents to children.

Meanwhile, in Aberdeen, a peaceful yet attention-
catching demonstration of Christmas spirit from
"oor Santie's" Dutch cousin, Saint Nicklaus, who
delighted shoppers and children during his
parade of Union Street with his traditional
Dutch entourage.

Arctic acres of frozen-over Dee between the
new Bridge of Dee and the railway bridge in the
winter of 1963.

Soggy dough from the Dee. A "Co-opie"
bakery van is retrieved after an unscheduled
plunge into the ice-floed river in 1965.
Sixties snows brought spates of suffering,
awkward to major on the news "Richter"
scale, most treated by the stoically-coping
Aberdonian as a "dam't nuisance".

Provost Ross's house in the Shiprow. Rising above it in the background is the spire of the Town House tower.

The most welcoming landmark of Aberdeen —
certainly for those approaching from the North
Sea — is Girdleness Lighthouse.

Aberdeen harbour in 1969 was busy still with
fish — not oil-related activity.

Market Day on the fish quay.

Mid-Sixties and a sparsely-populated harbour save for the visiting minesweeper, HMS Montrose of Tay Division, Royal Naval Reserve.

The oil "cuckoo" in the shape of an Esso vessel edges in, jostling the little native fishing vessels.

As the Sixties rolled to a close the unmistakable
shape of the oil rig derrick came to dominate
the harbour and the horizon from the shoreline
(opposite).

The Native

"So yer aff tae the eil,"
the aul' man said.
Robbie nodded aye,
stood stubborn by the bed
from where his father glimpsed the sky.

"An' fit dae ye ken o' dreels
by's neeps?"
said Father. Robbie sighed.
"Ah'm gan tae the eil-skweel, Dad,
tae learn the trade," he cried.

"An' will ye bide awa', son
till a' the eil's gan dry?
"Mither's deid an' Ah'll be aul' by 1975,
but yunger than the grun'
my fathers kept alive for me."

Robbie visited ere
twa year were oot, in his posh car
wi' foreign wife, gran' claes, a hoose in Tarves.

Father deid soon efter.

Griselda Sarah McGregor